THE·PARENT·AND·CHILD
·PROGRAMME·

Learning to Spell 2

Louis Fidge

Headteacher, Someries Junior School

Illustrated by Andy Cooke

ch

Mix likes ...

chicken and **ch**ips
and **ch**ocolate.

Max likes ...

lamb **ch**ops and
chips and **ch**erries.

Who likes **ch**erries?   M_____

Who likes **ch**icken?   _____

Who likes **ch**ips?   _____

Who likes lamb **ch**ops?   _____

In some words **ch** comes at the beginning. In some words
it comes at the end. Put these words into the correct bags.

~~chip~~   chicken   ~~much~~
rich   chat   lunch
pinch   chop   chest
march   chair   which
punch   chill   church

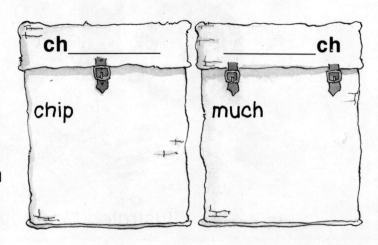

2

sh

Ring the **sh** words you can see in the picture.

shop   **sh**ock   **sh**ell   **sh**eep   **sh**ip   **sh**oot   **sh**ape

sharp   **sh**ark   sma**sh**   fre**sh**   fi**sh**   fla**sh**

Shoot out!

The **sh** has been **sh**ot out of these words. Can you put it back?

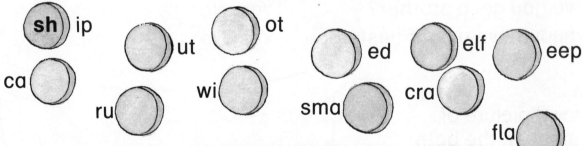

sh ip   ( ) ut   ( ) ot   ( ) ed   ( ) elf   ( ) eep

ca ( )   ru ( )   wi ( )   sma ( )   cra ( )

fla ( )

Choose the right **sh** word to finish these sentences.

The shop is _____. | shot | shut |

My _____ are too big for my feet. | shoes | ships |

I _____ my hair. | brush | bash |

The car was in a _____. | cash | crash |

3

th

Draw some jam on **the thin** slice of toast.

Draw some butter on **the thick** slice.

Tick yes or no.

Can a mo**th** fly? | Yes | No
Do you suck your **th**umb? | Yes | No
Are you **th**in? | Yes | No
Do you clean your tee**th**? | Yes | No
Do you like **th**under? | Yes | No
Is a **th**orn sharp? | Yes | No
Are you older **th**an **th**ree? | Yes | No
Have you got a bro**th**er? | Yes | No
Did you have a ba**th** yesterday? | Yes | No

Draw a picture of yourself in **the** ba**th**!

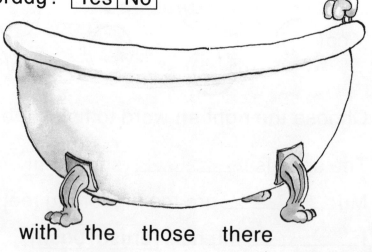

Ring **th** in each word.

mo(th)er   father   brother   with   the   those   there

then   this   that   them

4

wh

Who is the girl?

The girl's name is _____.

Where is she going?

She is _____.

Why is she going there?

She is _____.

What time is it?

It is _____.

whiskers   **wh**ale   **wh**eel   **wh**istle

Choose the right **wh** word from above to finish these sentences.

A _____ swims in the sea.

Cats have _____.

A _____ is round.

A referee blows a _____.

nd ng nk

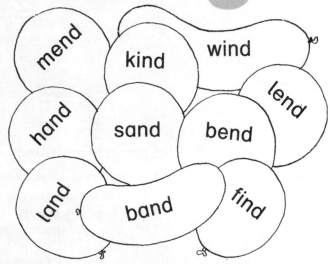

mend
kind
wind
lend
hand
sand
bend
land
band
find

Colour the **and** balloons red.
Colour the **end** balloons yellow.
Colour the **ind** balloons blue.

Tick the right word.

The bird | sing | sang |.

The bell | rang | ring |.

I sing a | sung | song |.

I won't be | long | lung |.

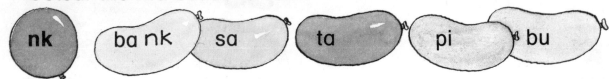

nk   ba nk   sa   ta   pi   bu

These words end with **nd**, **ng** and **nk**. Can you put them in the right shells?

nd   **ng**   **nk**

hand   **song**   **bank**

song grand lend long
hand bang   sunk
link   sing
bank bunk wind
   gang tank
      sand

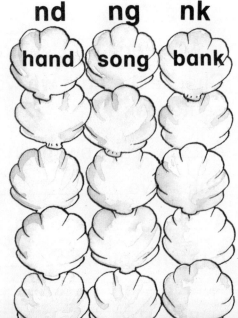

ll ss

Choose ll or ss
to finish these words.   A be __ __ rings.   Snakes hi__ __

Put the **ll** words in the **ll** monster.
Put the **ss** words in the **ss** monster.

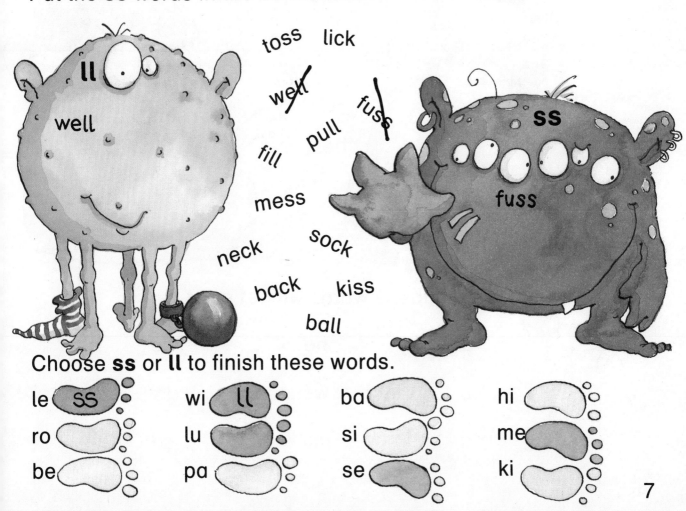

toss   lick

well

fuss

fill   pull

mess

neck   sock

back   kiss

ball

ll — well

ss — fuss

Choose **ss** or **ll** to finish these words.

le **ss**   wi **ll**   ba ___   hi ___
ro ___   lu ___   si ___   me ___
be ___   pa ___   se ___   ki ___

7

st nt

Choose st or nt
to finish these words.

a _ _ ne _ _

Put the st words in
Max's sack.

Put the nt words in Mix's sack.

pant   sent   lost
rest   fast
list   grunt
dent
best
tent

st

lost

nt

sent

Finish these words with st or nt.

a *n* *t*   ne *s* *t*   de _ _

co _ _   we _ _   lo _ _

pa _ _   mu _ _   se _ _

8

ck mp

quack!

A du**ck** can swim.

A kangaroo can ju**mp**.

Write the **mp** words on the camel's hu**mp**.

Write the **ck** words on the camel's sa**ck**.

mp
dump

ck
stick

sock   rock

lick

ramp

dump

luck

bump

stick   pump

deck

lamp

ck	Put on the best
mp	sta**mp** to finish these words.

bu ▢   lo ▢   si ▢

ki ▢   li ▢   ju ▢

9

a-e

whale

I am a snake.

gate

spade

What am I?

You open me. I am a g _ _ _.
I swim in the sea. I am a w _ _ _ _.
I hiss. I am a sn _ _ _.
You dig with me. I am a sp _ _ _.

a	b	m	a	k	e	c	s	a	v	e
d	e	f	g	s	k	a	t	e	h	i
t	a	k	e	k	l	m	a	t	m	o
h	a	t	s	b	r	a	v	e	f	j
l	g	a	v	e	n	t	m	a	d	e
a	t	h	a	t	e	p	c	a	m	e
n	a	m	e	r	l	a	t	e	s	t

Fill in the missing letters **a-e**.

pl **a** _ t e   l _ k _

m _ k _   g _ m _

l _ t _   s _ f _

c _ v _   t _ m _

Can you find these **a-e** words in the puzzle?

| late | hate | take | name | skate | brave |
| make | made | gave | came | save | |

10

i-e

kit**e**

slid**e**

bik**e**

k__t__   b__k__   sl__d__

Answer yes or no.

Can you r**i**d**e** a b**i**k**e**? _____

Can you dr**i**v**e** a car? _____

Can you tell the t**i**m**e**? _____

Can you sl**i**d**e** on **i**ce? _____

Do you sm**i**l**e** a lot? _____

Throw a ring on to the **i-e** in each word.

i-e

mile   ripe   fine   bite   prize   pile

like   wipe   five   shine

dice   mine   nine   side

white

11

o-e

Choose the right **o-e** words to finish these sentences.

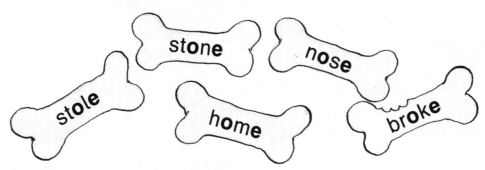

I smell with my _____.

The girl threw a _____ and _____ a window.

After school I go _____.

The thief _____ some money.

Finish these words with **o-e**.

b__n__   h__m__   h__l__   sp__k__

n__t__   j__k__   r__p__   br__k__

12

u-e

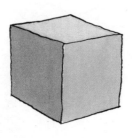

c__b__   t__b__

u-e

Stop Max! Put the stolen **u-e** letters back into each of these words.

t**u**b**e**   c__b__   t__n__

fl__t__   c__t__   r__d__

Find the **u-e** words on the cube. Write them here.

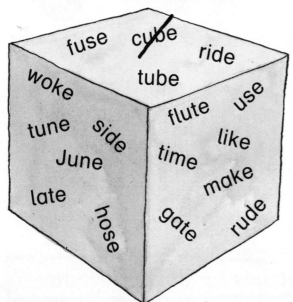

cube

_____

_____

_____

_____

_____

_____

13

bl cl fl

Colour the flag **bl**ue.
Colour the **cl**own's hat red.
Colour the **fl**owers yellow.

Choose the best words from below to
finish these sentences.

This _____ tells the time.

You can see _____ in the sky.

A candle burns with a _____ .

The car tyre was _____ .

You have to _____ up balloons.

There was a _____ of lightning.

| flame | blow | clock | clouds | flash | flat |

gl pl sl

Fill the **gl**ass with orange.

Draw Mix on the **sl**ide.

Draw Max **pl**aying on the swing.

Colour these **gl**, **pl** or **sl** words in the puzzle.

slippers   **sl**eep   **sl**ap

slot   **gl**ad   **gl**ue

plate   **pl**um   **pl**ay

gloves

a	g	l	u	e	b	c	s	l	e	e	p
s	l	o	t	d	p	l	a	t	e	f	g
h	i	l	g	l	a	d	l	y	m	n	o
r	p	l	u	m	s	t	p	l	a	y	w
y	e	s	g	l	o	v	e	s	f	l	y
g	l	e	n	d	o	n	s	l	a	p	e
p	s	l	i	p	p	e	r	s	p	l	y

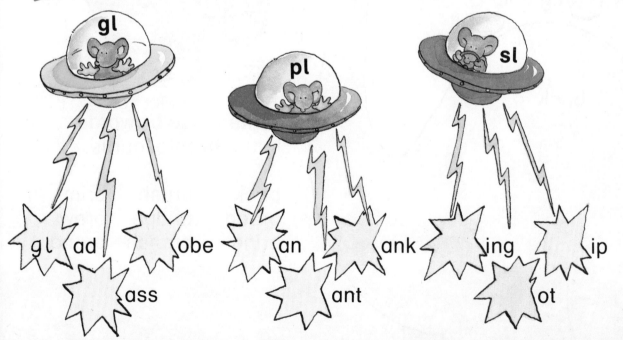

gl ad   obe   an   ank   ing   ip

ass   ant   ot

15

br cr dr

I'm **Cr**uncher the **cr**ocodile. I was hungry so I ate all the **cr** letters in these words. Can you put them back for me?

cr ab | own | ack | ash | isp | ust

Hi! I'm **Dr**ax the **dr**agon. I was thirsty so I **dr**ank all the **dr** letters!

dr um | ip | op | ess | ag | ill

brick

Write these **br** words in the **br**ontosaurus.

~~brick~~   brush   brim
bread   bridge   brew
bring   branch   brand

gr pr tr

Max gave Mix
a **pr**esent.

Max **gr**inned when
Mix opened the box.

It was a **tr**ick.

gr

g r ab
__ __ im
__ __ ip
__ __ unt

pr

__ __ esent
__ __ od
__ __ int

tr

__ __ actor
__ __ uck
__ __ ap
__ __ ick

Colour the right word.

Mix tried to | grub | grab | Max.

Mix played a | trick | trap | on Max.

Max is driving the | grain | train |.

Max is blowing a | trumpet | crumpet |.

Mix is eating a | green | preen | lolly.

17

sc sm sp

Winnie the witch and **Sp**ook the **sp**ider are weaving a magic **sp**ell.

Tick the things you think Winnie might need.

scales ☐   **sp**ear ☐

smoke ☐   **sp**ade ☐

spoon ☐   **sm**ash ☐

spin ☐   **sp**ot ☐

smell ☐   **sc**ar ☐

Look at this page from Winnie's spell book. Some of the letters have disappeared. Finish the spell by writing **sm** or **sp** in the gaps.

If you want to make a spell
Mix these up and stir them well.

2 **sm**all bats,

A _ _ aceman's toe nail,

2 _ _ ots from a dice,

A _ _ ile from a clown's face,

The _ _ oke from a fire,

And the point of a _ _ ear.

18

sk sw

Tick the word if you can find it in the picture.

skirt	☐	**sk**ull	☐
skate	☐	**sw**an	☐
sky	☐	**sw**itch	☐
skid	☐	**sw**eeping	☐
skipping	☐	**sw**ings	☐
skill	☐	**sw**ell	☐

sk or sw?

s w eets   _ _ eep

_ _ ip   _ _ itch

_ _ ate   _ _ id

_ _ ill   _ _ irt

_ _ im

19

sn st

Choose **sn** or **st** to finish these words.

The __ __ ail is on the __ __ ool.

The __ __ ake is on the __ __ airs.

sn	st
snow	stamp

These words are mixed up. Can you sort them out for me?

~~stamp~~	stand	sting
~~snow~~	snap	sneeze
step	snort	stung
stab	stop	snow
sniff	steam	stamp
stick	snip	

Choose the best words to finish these sentences.

snowing

_____ the _____ on the envelope.

It is so cold it is _____.

A bee _____.

When I have a cold I _____ and _____.

stings

sniff

stick

sneeze

stamp

20

ay

Sunday	1 2 3 4
Monday	5 6 7 8
Tuesday	9 10 11 12
Wednesday	13 14 15 16
Thursday	17 18 19 20
Friday	21 22 23 24
Saturday	25 26 27 28

Help!

How many mugs
are on the tr**ay**?

What is Mix s**ay**ing?

What d**ay** is it tod**ay?**

_____

_____

It is _____.

d a y   ay

p _ _   ay

r _ _ _   ay

pl _ _ _   ay

st _ _ _   ay

aw _ _ _   ay

s _ _ _ _   ay

cl _ _ _   ay

h _ _   ay

        ay

        ay

Finish these sentences.

There are seven _ _ _ _ _ in a week.

_ _ _ _ is the name of a month.

Horses eat _ _ _ _ .

Colour the **ay** words in this puzzle.

b	d	a	y	c	d	m	a	y
e	f	s	a	y	h	i	k	l
h	a	y	m	n	p	a	y	p
r	s	w	a	y	t	l	a	y
v	x	y	m	r	a	y	b	d
p	l	a	y	d	e	f	t	l
b	c	e	f	g	a	w	a	y

21

ee

Finish the words on the **tree** with **ee**.
Then write them here.

b _e e_

f ___ t

d ___ p

p ___ t

cr ___ p

sw ___ t

bl ___ d

st ___ p

b ___ n

gr ___ n

n ___ d

w ___ k

bee _____

_____

_____

_____

_____

_____

_____

_____

_____

_____

_____

Some of these **ee** words rhyme with sh**ee**p.
Write them in the sheep.

sheep

weep

see	deep
weep	steep
seek	keen
keep	creep
bleed	week
need	seem
sweet	been

oo

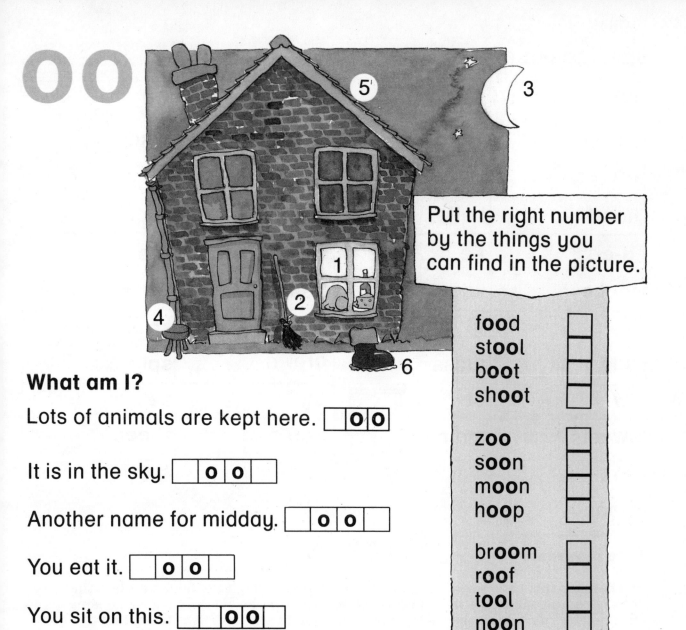

Put the right number by the things you can find in the picture.

What am I?

Lots of animals are kept here. □ **o o**

It is in the sky. □ **o** □ **o** □

Another name for midday. □ **o** □ **o** □

You eat it. □ **o** □ **o** □

You sit on this. □ □ **o o** □

food □
stool □
boot □
shoot □

zoo □
soon □
moon □
hoop □

broom □
roof □
tool □
noon □

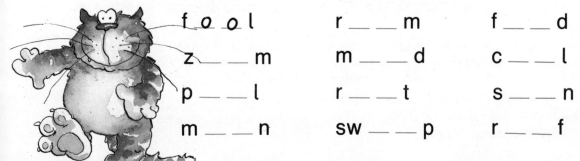

Finish these words with **oo.**

f _o_ _o_ l	r _ _ m	f _ _ d
z _ _ m	m _ _ d	c _ _ l
p _ _ l	r _ _ t	s _ _ n
m _ _ n	sw _ _ p	r _ _ f

23

Spelling patterns

ch chicken	sh ship	th bath	wh whale
nd hand	ll bell	nt tent	ck sock
a-e snake	i-e kite	o-e bone	u-e cube
fl flag	gl glass	cr crown	sp spider
sw sweets	st stamp	ay tray	ee sheep
oo moon			

Note to Parents

You can use this page while your child is working through the book or when the book is completed. It is a way of revising or checking the spelling patterns being learnt. This chart does cover all the main spelling patterns in the book. Don't worry that every individual spelling pattern is not represented here.

Look at one of the pictures. Say what it is. Look at the word. Say the word. Point out the coloured letters to your child. Look carefully again at the word together. Next, cover the word. Now ask your child to write it from memory. Uncover the word and get your child to check the spelling. If it is wrong discuss the mistake, then have another go.

Do this one word at a time. Don't try to do too many words at once. Make sure your child can remember how to write each word on different occasions. When your child can write the word correctly several times, colour in the relevant picture as a record of progress.

Remember – speaking clearly, looking, listening and writing carefully, are all important aspects of spelling.